Intro to
SOAP

A GUIDE TO MAKING THE BIBLE COME TO LIFE!

Wayne Cordeiro wrote a book, the *Divine Mentor,* which introduced this wonderful and simple process of studying the Bible that we know of as SOAP. Used by permission.

Printed in the United States of America

First Printing, 2012

ISBN 978-0-9829252-2-5

Published by
next level
CHURCH

www.nextlevelchurch.com

how to use this book

Welcome to a new and great adventure! Your decision to learn more about SOAP and study the Bible will have an incredible impact on your life and your relationship with the living God! This book is for you to use, write in, and interact with. Inside, you'll find Scriptures, explanations, and "QR codes" to companion videos that can be watched on the internet. Any time you see a code, you can use your smart phone to scan the code, and your phone will automatically take you to a video that corresponds to that day's SOAP.

If you do not have a smart phone, simply type the web site listed under each code into your internet browser to watch the video.

If you have a smart phone, here are some simple instructions on how to download and use a QR Reader.

1. Go to the App Store on your phone and search for a free QR Code Reader.
2. Download the QR Reader to your phone.
3. When you come to a QR code in this book, take out your phone and open the QR Reader App that you downloaded.
4. Point your phone's camera at the QR code, and the phone will redirect you to the video.

introduction to the Bible

When we ask people, "Do you read the Bible?" one of the most common answers is, "I would, but I don't because I don't understand what it means."

We believe that the Bible is the inspired word of God for us. This being true, it is so important that we actually read and understand it! To think that God may actually speak to us through encountering His word is an awesome thought.

This book is intended to help you learn a way to read and study the Bible that will enable you to see that it really is God's word for *you*.

The Bible is not just one big book but a collection of sixty-six smaller books written over a period of at least sixteen hundred years by about forty different authors. Everything they wrote was inspired by God.

In the front of your Bible is a table of contents, which lists the names of all the books in the Bible. The Bible is divided into two sections. The first section, which contains three-fourths of the Bible is the Old Testament; the second section is the New Testament.

The Old Testament reveals to us how God dealt with the nation of Israel. It looks forward to the coming Savior of the world, Jesus. Beginning with the book of Genesis and ending with Malachi, the Old Testament is divided into four general areas:

1. The first five books (Genesis to Deuteronomy) tell us the beginning of man and the establishment of the nation of Israel with the promise of the Savior of the world coming from this chosen people. It not only contains the early history of Israel, but also the Law of God as revealed through Moses. For example, Exodus chapter 20 records the Ten Commandments.
2. The next twelve books (Joshua to Esther) are the historical books of the nation of Israel after it became a kingdom in a land called Canaan.
3. The next five books (Job to Song of Solomon) are the books of poetry and wisdom in the Bible. Especially helpful to new believers are the book of Psalms, which was the hymnal or songbook of the nation of Israel, and Proverbs, which contains the sayings and advice of Solomon, the wisest king of Israel.
4. The last seventeen books (Isaiah to Malachi) are the books of the prophets of Israel whom God sent to warn, admonish, and encourage his people toward the end of the history of Israel as a nation.

The New Testament introduces us to Jesus and the plan of salvation. It begins with the book of Matthew and ends with the book of Revelation. It is divided into four general sections:

1. The first four books: Matthew, Mark, Luke, and John tell us the story of Jesus when he was on this earth.

2. The book of Acts tells us the history of the early church after Jesus' death and resurrection.
3. The letters (from Romans to Jude) are correspondence from early Christian leaders to other churches or individuals.
4. Finally, the book of Revelation tells us the future story of the end time when Jesus will come back to this world and reign on earth.

There is a handy abbreviation that is used to specify verses in the Bible. It starts with the name of the book first, followed by the chapter number, and then the verse number. For example, John 3:16 means the book of John, chapter 3, verse 16. This way you can quickly and easily locate Scriptures.

SOAP is an acronym for how to study the Bible.

S stands for Scripture. It all starts when you read the Bible, whether it is a verse or chapter. When you read the Bible, pay attention to what verse or phrase really stands out to you. Feel free to underline in your Bible as you read; this will help you identify meaningful verses or phrases. Once you identify what stands out the most, write it down.

O stands for Observation. This part is as simple as writing down what you think the verse or phrase means. Don't worry about getting this exactly right; that is not the point. The most important part of this is beginning to interact with the Bible.

A stands for Application. Once you write down what you think the verse means, take the next step and write down how you think the verse applies to your life. This is where we take the word of God and make it personal.

P stands for Prayer. The last step in the process is to take your application and write out a prayer of how you want God to make it real in your life.

In the pages to follow is a step-by-step process that teaches you how to SOAP and how to interact the Bible.

This process will begin with bite-sized verses that will make it easy to learn the process of SOAPing. We will then start to look at small stories and passages and eventually build up to full chapters. Once you finish this book, you will have the skills necessary to grab a SOAP Reading Guide and pick up with the chapter of the day that the entire church is following.

We are excited that you will be interacting with God and his word, the Bible, as you SOAP!

day one

Proverbs 3:5, 6

Welcome to day one of SOAP. We are so glad that you are going through the process of learning to SOAP and learning to interact with God's word, the Bible. The first passage we are going to look at is from a book in the Bible called Proverbs. This is a book of wise sayings that, even though they were written thousands of years ago, are

www.nextlevelchurch.com/day1

still amazingly applicable for our lives today. When you write out your SOAP, don't worry about getting things, "right" or perfect. This has more to do with you interacting with the Bible than anything else. On the next page you will find a sample SOAP for day one. This sample is not the only right way to do a SOAP; it is just an example of a personal encounter with the Bible. We hope you enjoy this time with God's word.

Proverbs 3:5,6 encapsulates the goal for all of us as followers of Christ.

Proverbs 3:5, 6 5Trust in the LORD with all your heart and lean not on your own understanding; 6in all your ways submit to him, and he will make your paths straight.

9

Sample SOAP—day 1

Scripture: (the verse or phrase that stands out to you)
Proverbs 3:5 Trust in the Lord with all your heart.

Observation: (what you think this verse means)
God wants me to trust Him with every area of my life.

Application: (how it affects you or applies to your life)
I don't always trust God with everything. I tend to have trouble trusting God with things I like to control, like finances or relationships.

Prayer: (asking God to help you live out this verse)
God, I struggle with trusting you in certain areas. Please help me, especially with my financial life and my relationships.

Your SOAP—day 1

Scripture: _____

_____

_____

_____

Observation: _____

_____

_____

_____

_____

Application: _____

_____

_____

_____

_____

Prayer: _____

_____

_____

_____

_____

This may be the most recognized verse in the Bible. In one verse, the story of the Bible is contained in a single phrase. The verse to follow is also very powerful but tends to get lost in the shadow of John 3:16's popularity. It is one of those passages where we begin to realize God's motivation and what our intended response should be. The gift that God gives through his Son Jesus Christ, and our belief in his Son, results in eternal life and relationship with God. That's an awesome thing! This is also the passage from which Christians gain the word "saved." This word is used to describe the encounter of putting our faith and trust in Jesus Christ.

www.nextlevelchurch.com/day2

Just so you know. These verses are written by John, one of Christ's followers. He wrote one of four books that are all about the life of Jesus. These books are called the Gospels. Another name for the book of John is the gospel of John.

John 3:16, 17 16For God so loved the world that he gave his one and only Son, that whoever believes in him shall not perish but have eternal life. 17For God did not send his Son into the world to condemn the world, but to save the world through him.

Sample SOAP—day 2

Scripture:
John 3:16 Whoever believes in him shall not perish but have eternal life.

Observation:
God says that whoever believes or puts their faith in Jesus will live forever.

Application:
When I put my faith and belief in Jesus I can now live because of him.

Prayer:
God, I put my faith in your Son Jesus.

Your SOAP—day 2

Scripture: _____

_____

_____

_____

Observation: _____

_____

_____

_____

Application: _____

_____

_____

_____

Prayer: _____

_____

_____

_____

day three

Ephesians 2:8, 9

Today's verse is a great passage that talks a little more about this salvation experience of putting our faith and trust in Jesus Christ. With this verse, we introduce a very important word, "grace." A simple definition of grace is unearned favor. So when you read and SOAP on this verse, pay attention to the emphasis on grace. This is also one of

www.nextlevelchurch.com/day3

those verses in the Bible where we start to see that salvation, and relationship with God, is not based on being good enough; it is only because God loves us so much that he looks on us with favor, even when we don't deserve it.

Ephesians 2:8, 9 8For it is by grace you have been saved, through faith—and this is not from yourselves, it is the gift of God—9not by works, so that no one can boast.

Sample SOAP—day 3

S: *Ephesians 2:9 Not by works, so that no one can boast.*

O: *Being saved is about grace and faith. It is not about me being good enough. If we could be good enough, then we would probably brag about it.*

A: *I know that I will never be good enough for God to save me, but I am so thankful that his grace saves me.*

P: *God, thank you so much for saving me when I know there is no way for me to save myself. Help me to continue to put my faith in you.*

Your SOAP—day 3

Scripture: _____

_____

_____

_____

Observation: _____

_____

_____

_____

_____

Application: _____

_____

_____

_____

_____

Prayer: _____

_____

_____

_____

_____

_____

day four
Romans 10:9, 10

This is another one of the more memorable verses in the Bible that answers the simple question, "So how do I get saved?" The Bible is not all about fulfilling a

www.nextlevelchurch.com/day4

formula so that we can have relationship with God, and God certainly isn't looking for people who will just complete a required list of "to do's." However, for those of us that need a very clear place to start, these verses in Romans are it.

One more thing about these verses. There is a word in verse ten that doesn't make its way into our modern vocabulary very often. The word is "justified." To be justified is to declare innocent or guiltless, absolve, or acquit.

This word in this verse gives us even greater insight into our relationship with God.

When you read the Bible and come across a word that you are not familiar with, don't be afraid to look it up. Knowing what everything means is a huge part of making the Bible more understandable when we read it.

Definition—Justified: to declare innocent or guilt-less, absolve, acquit.

Romans 10:9, 10 ⁹If you declare with your mouth, "Jesus is Lord," and believe in your heart that God raised him from the dead, you will be saved. [10]For it is with your heart that you believe and are justified, and it is with your mouth that you profess your faith and are saved.

Sample SOAP—day 4

S: *Romans 10:10 For it is with your heart that you believe and are justified, and it is with your mouth that you profess your faith and are saved.*

O: *Belief starts with the heart. If your heart is not in it, it doesn't seem to matter. We can just say something and not believe it. Words without belief don't make a difference. Salvation is saying and believing. When this happens, we are declared innocent by God from all the mistakes in our past.*

A: *God wants my heart, not just my words or actions. God wants my relationship with him to be authentic.*

P: *God, I give you my heart and I choose to follow you. And because of this, I declare that you are my Lord and Savior.*

Your SOAP—day 4

Scripture: _____

_____

_____

_____

Observation: _____

_____

_____

_____

_____

Application: _____

_____

_____

_____

_____

Prayer: _____

_____

_____

_____

_____

day five

Today we are going to continue to introduce some new words. Even though you may be familiar with this word, it is important to make sure that we have at least given a definition for it. The word is "sin."

www.nextlevelchurch.com/day5

For us, sin includes anything we have ever done that has gone against God's desire or plan for us.

Certainly, the thought of listing out every sin we may have ever committed is very overwhelming and brings with it much guilt and shame.

Yet even in our guilt and shame, God's love shines through, especially in this passage.

Definition—Sin: any act regarded as a transgression, especially a willful or deliberate violation of some religious or moral principle.

Definition—Righteousness: to be morally upright or to be in right standing with God.

1 John 1:9 9If we confess our sins, he is faithful and just and will forgive us our sins and purify us from all unrighteousness.

Did you notice? The word confess was also in the previous day's SOAP.

21

Sample SOAP—day 5

S: *1 John 1:9 If we confess our sins, he is faithful and just to forgive us our sins and purify us from all righteousness.*

O: *When we confess or ask God for forgiveness from the mistakes and sins in our life, God will always forgive us and then wash our hearts clean from those sins.*

A: *This all starts with me confessing my sin to God, but then after that, God not only forgives me, no matter what, but he then purifies my otherwise impure heart.*

P: *God, I confess my sin to you now and I ask for forgiveness. My heart has been impure and my motives, attitudes, and decisions have been wrong. Please forgive me. God, I thank you so much that you do forgive me and now are washing my heart to make it clean and pure.*

Your SOAP—day 5

Scripture: _____

_____

_____

_____

Observation: _____

_____

_____

_____

Application: _____

_____

_____

_____

Prayer: _____

_____

_____

_____

_____

day six

2 Corinthians 12:9

Today we will look at another verse that talks about grace. This is a powerful passage written by one of the main authors of the New Testament, the apostle Paul.

www.nextlevelchurch.com/day6

Before he had his life-changing salvation experience, he used to persecute the early Christians. There is also a good chance that he was responsible for Christians losing their lives. So if there was ever a person to be overwhelmed with guilt and regret and shortcomings in life, it was this guy. Yet this passage is actually a word that God spoke to Paul as he faced his own insecurities. Keep this in mind as you read and do your SOAP on this great verse of 2 Corinthians 12:9.

2 Corinthians 12:9 9But he said to me, "My grace is sufficient for you, for my power is made perfect in weakness." Therefore I will boast all the more gladly about my weaknesses, so that Christ's power may rest on me.

Sample SOAP—day 6

S: *2 Corinthians 12:9 "My grace is sufficient for you, for my power is made perfect in weakness." Therefore I will boast all the more gladly about my weaknesses, so that Christ's power may rest on me.*

O: *God's grace, or unearned favor, is for us, even in our continual weaknesses. God can actually shine through our weaknesses because it will be proof that it is him working instead of us.*

A: *To think that God not only doesn't judge me for my weaknesses, but that he covers them with so much unearned favor that they may actually look like strengths. Anytime that God could possibly use a weakness of mine to make it a strength, that is nothing short of a miracle. Thank you, God!*

P: *God, I have so many weaknesses and faults. I thank you so much that you are able to use them as an avenue to bring your strength. I invite you into my areas of weakness because that is where I need the help the most in my life.*

Your SOAP—day 6

Scripture: _____

_____

_____

_____

Observation: _____

_____

_____

_____

Application: _____

_____

_____

_____

Prayer: _____

_____

_____

_____

_____

day seven
Romans 5:1–8

Up until now we have been getting comfortable with doing a SOAP on a verse or two. This time we are taking a step up and looking at an entire passage. As you read this passage of eight verses, pay attention to what verse or phrase stands out to you the most and do your SOAP on that verse.

www.nextlevelchurch.com/day7

Don't forget all the definitions we have looked at so far because this passage puts them all together.

Romans 5:1–8 1Therefore, since we have been justified through faith, we have peace with God through our Lord Jesus Christ, 2through whom we have gained access by faith into this grace in which we now stand. And we boast in the hope of the glory of God. 3Not only so, but we also glory in our sufferings, because we know that suffering produces perseverance; 4perseverance, character; and character, hope. 5And hope does not put us to shame, because God's love has been poured out into our hearts through the Holy Spirit, who has been given to us. 6You see, at just the right time, when we were still powerless, Christ died for the ungodly. 7Very rarely will anyone die for a righteous person, though for a good person someone

27

might possibly dare to die. [8]But God demonstrates his own love for us in this: While we were still sinners, Christ died for us.

Sample SOAP—day 7

S: *Romans 5:8 But God demonstrates his own love for us in this: While we were still sinners, Christ died for us.*

O: *God showed his love for us first. He sent his Son to save us even while we were in our own sin. He died for us.*

A: *I have always had a hard time maintaining a friendship with someone that messes up time and time again, but think that God did this for me . . . wow!*

P: *Thank you, God, for pursuing me, knowing that I have never deserved it.*

Your SOAP—day 7

Scripture: _____

_____

_____

_____

Observation: _____

_____

_____

_____

_____

Application: _____

_____

_____

_____

_____

Prayer: _____

_____

_____

_____

_____

_____

29

Romans 8:31–39 31What, then, shall we say in response to these things? If God is for us, who can be against us? 32He who did not spare his own Son, but gave him up for us all—how will he not also, along with him, graciously give us all things? 33Who will bring any charge against those whom God has chosen? It is God who justifies. 34Who then is the one who condemns? No one. Christ Jesus who died—more than that, who was raised to life—is at the right hand of God and is also interceding for us. 35Who shall separate us from the love of Christ? Shall trouble or hardship or persecution or famine or nakedness or danger or sword? 36As it is written: "For your sake we face death all day long; we are considered as sheep to be slaughtered." 37No, in all these things we are more than conquerors through him who loved us. 38For I am convinced that neither death nor life, neither angels nor demons, neither the present nor the future, nor any powers, 39neither height nor depth, nor anything else in all creation, will be able to separate us from the love of God that is in Christ Jesus our Lord.

Your SOAP—day 8

Scripture: _____

_____

_____

_____

Observation: _____

_____

_____

_____

_____

Application: _____

_____

_____

_____

_____

Prayer: _____

_____

_____

_____

_____

_____

Philippians 4:4–9 4Rejoice in the Lord always. I will say it again: Rejoice! 5Let your gentleness be evident to all. The Lord is near. 6Do not be anxious about anything, but in every situation, by prayer and petition, with thanksgiving, present your requests to God. 7And the peace of God, which transcends all understanding, will guard your hearts and your minds in Christ Jesus. 8Finally, brothers and sisters, whatever is true, whatever is noble, whatever is right, whatever is pure, whatever is lovely, whatever is admirable—if anything is excellent or praiseworthy—think about such things. 9Whatever you have learned or received or heard from me, or seen in me—put it into practice. And the God of peace will be with you.

Your SOAP—day 9

Scripture: _____

_____

_____

_____

Observation: _____

_____

_____

_____

_____

Application: _____

_____

_____

_____

_____

Prayer: _____

_____

_____

_____

_____

Wₑ are so glad that you have made it this far and are continuing to interact with the Bible as you SOAP. In the passage we are about to look at, we are

www.nextlevelchurch.com/day10

getting our first glimpse into the early days of the first Christians. The book we are in is the book of Acts, which is an historical book that describes the early Christian church after the death and resurrection of Jesus Christ. Even though this is an early description of what church life was like, there is so much that applies to us today.

Acts 2:42–47 42They devoted themselves to the apostles' teaching and to fellowship, to the breaking of bread and to prayer. 43Everyone was filled with awe at the many wonders and signs performed by the apostles. 44All the believers were together and had everything in common. 45They sold property and possessions to give to anyone who had need. 46Every day they continued to meet together in the temple courts. They broke bread in their homes and ate together with glad and sincere hearts, 47praising God and enjoying the favor of all the people. And the Lord added to their number daily those who were being saved.

Your SOAP—day 10

Scripture: _____

_____

_____

_____

_____

Observation: _____

_____

_____

_____

_____

Application: _____

_____

_____

_____

_____

Prayer: _____

_____

_____

_____

_____

_____

day eleven
Matthew 6:5–15

This is a passage from Matthew, one of the four gospels or stories of the life of Jesus Christ. In this passage, Jesus is teaching his disciples on the topic of prayer.

www.nextlevelchurch.com/day11

Matthew 6:5–15 5"And when you pray, do not be like the hypocrites, for they love to pray standing in the synagogues and on the street corners to be seen by others. Truly I tell you, they have received their reward in full. 6But when you pray, go into your room, close the door and pray to your Father, who is unseen. Then your Father, who sees what is done in secret, will reward you. 7And when you pray, do not keep on babbling like pagans, for they think they will be heard because of their many words. 8Do not be like them, for your Father knows what you need before you ask him.9This, then, is how you should pray: 'Our Father in heaven, hallowed be your name, 10your kingdom come, your will be done, on earth as it is in heaven. 11Give us today our daily bread. 12And forgive us our debts, as we also have forgiven our debtors. 13And lead us not into temptation, but deliver us from the evil one.' 14For if you forgive other people when they sin against you, your heavenly Father will also forgive you. [15]But if you do not forgive others their sins, your Father will not forgive your sins."

Your SOAP—day 11

Scripture: _____

_____

_____

Observation: _____

_____

_____

_____

Application: _____

_____

_____

_____

Prayer: _____

_____

_____

_____

Today's passage is a continuation of Jesus' teachings that we SOAPed about yesterday.

www.nextlevelchurch.com/day12

Matthew 6:25–34 25"Therefore I tell you, do not worry about your life, what you will eat or drink; or about your body, what you will wear. Is not life more than food, and the body more than clothes? 26Look at the birds of the air; they do not sow or reap or store away in barns, and yet your heavenly Father feeds them. Are you not much more valuable than they? 27Can any one of you by worrying add a single hour to your life? 28And why do you worry about clothes? See how the flowers of the field grow. They do not labor or spin. 29Yet I tell you that not even Solomon in all his splendor was dressed like one of these. 30If that is how God clothes the grass of the field, which is here today and tomorrow is thrown into the fire, will he not much more clothe you—you of little faith? 31So do not worry, saying, 'What shall we eat?' or 'What shall we drink?' or 'What shall we wear?' 32For the pagans run after all these things, and your heavenly Father knows that you need them. 33But seek first his kingdom and his righteousness, and all these things will be given to you as well. 34Therefore do not worry about tomorrow, for tomorrow will worry about itself. Each day has enough trouble of its own."

Your SOAP—day 12

Scripture: _____

_____

_____

_____

Observation: _____

_____

_____

_____

Application: _____

_____

_____

_____

Prayer: _____

_____

_____

_____

day thirteen
Matthew 14:22–32

Today we have one of the most famous true stories involving Jesus and his disciples. It is a story of faith, trust, and keeping your eyes on God.

www.nextlevelchurch.com/day13

Just to give you a little context, Jesus had just finished a very big day of preaching to a huge group of people. To end his day, Jesus was wanting a little alone time from the crowds and his followers, the disciples, to pray.

Pay attention to how you relate to this story and the characters in it. We trust that God will speak to you through this wonderful story.

Matthew 14:22–32 22Immediately Jesus made the disciples get into the boat and go on ahead of him to the other side, while he dismissed the crowd. 23After he had dismissed them, he went up on a mountainside by himself to pray. Later that night, he was there alone, 24and the boat was already a considerable distance from land, buffeted by the waves because the wind was against it. 25Shortly before dawn Jesus went out to them, walking on the lake. 26When the disciples saw him walking on the lake, they were terrified. "It's a ghost," they said, and cried out in fear.

27But Jesus immediately said to them: "Take courage! It is I. Don't be afraid."

28"Lord, if it's you," Peter replied, "tell me to come to you on the water."

29"Come," he said. Then Peter got down out of the boat, walked on the water and came toward Jesus. 30But when he saw the wind, he was afraid and, beginning to sink, cried out, "Lord, save me!"

31Immediately Jesus reached out his hand and caught him. "You of little faith," he said, "why did you doubt?" 32And when they climbed into the boat, the wind died down.

Sample SOAP—day 13

S: *Matthew 14:30 But when he saw the wind, he was afraid and, beginning to sink, cried out, "Lord, save me!"*

O: *When Peter saw the storm and stopped looking at Jesus, he began to sink and then he cried out to Jesus.*

A: *So often when I go through a difficult time in my life (bills stacking up, sickness, family struggles), I tend to take my attention off Christ instead of focusing on him.*

P: *God, please help me to focus on you when I go through the storms of life. I thank you that you really are always there to save me.*

Scripture: _____

_____

_____

_____

Observation: _____

_____

_____

_____

Application: _____

_____

_____

_____

Prayer: _____

_____

_____

_____

_____

In this passage in the gospel of Luke, we are going to look at a kind of teaching story that Jesus would tell in order to explain a principle of God. These teaching stories are called parables, and Jesus used them often while he was speaking.

www.nextlevelchurch.com/day14

This parable of the good Samaritan has many wonderful principles to teach.

Just so you know. Samaritans were a group of people that most Jews of the day had no contact with and avoided at all costs. The Jews considered the Samaritans not true Jews because they had, in their past, married non-Jews.

Enjoy this wonderful parable.

Luke 10:25–37 25On one occasion an expert in the law stood up to test Jesus. "Teacher," he asked, "What must I do to inherit eternal life?"

26"What is written in the Law?" he replied. "How do you read it?"

27He answered, "'Love the Lord your God with all your heart and with all your soul and with all your strength and with all your mind'; and, 'Love your neighbor as yourself.'"

28"You have answered correctly," Jesus replied. "Do this and you will live."

29But he wanted to justify himself, so he asked Jesus, "And who is my neighbor?"

30In reply Jesus said: "A man was going down from Jerusalem to Jericho, when he was attacked by robbers. They stripped him of his clothes, beat him and went away, leaving him half dead. 31A priest happened to be going down the same road, and when he saw the man, he passed by on the other side. 32So too, a Levite, when he came to the place and saw him, passed by on the other side. 33But a Samaritan, as he traveled, came where the man was; and when he saw him, he took pity on him. 34He went to him and bandaged his wounds, pouring on oil and wine. Then he put the man on his own donkey, brought him to an inn and took care of him. 35The next day he took out two denarii and gave them to the innkeeper. 'Look after him,' he said, 'and when I return, I will reimburse you for any extra expense you may have.'

36"Which of these three do you think was a neighbor to the man who fell into the hands of robbers?"

37The expert in the law replied, "The one who had mercy on him."

Jesus told him, "Go and do likewise."

Your SOAP—day 14

Scripture: _____

_____

_____

_____

Observation: _____

_____

_____

_____

_____

Application: _____

_____

_____

_____

_____

Prayer: _____

_____

_____

_____

_____

_____

Here is another famous teaching parable that Jesus uses to help us see the love and grace of God. This is the parable of the Prodigal Son.

www.nextlevelchurch.com/day15

Luke 15:11–32 ¹¹Jesus continued: "There was a man who had two sons. ¹²The younger one said to his father, 'Father, give me my share of the estate'. So he divided his property between them.

¹³"Not long after that, the younger son got together all he had, set off for a distant country and there squandered his wealth in wild living. ¹⁴After he had spent everything, there was a severe famine in that whole country, and he began to be in need. ¹⁵So he went and hired himself out to a citizen of that country, who sent him to his fields to feed pigs. ¹⁶He longed to fill his stomach with the pods that the pigs were eating, but no one gave him anything.

¹⁷"When he came to his senses, he said, 'How many of my father's hired servants have food to spare, and here I am starving to death! ¹⁸I will set out and go back to my father and say to him: "Father, I have sinned against heaven and against you. ¹⁹I am no longer worthy to be called your son; make me like one of your hired servants."' ²⁰So he got up and went

46

to his father. But while he was still a long way off, his father saw him and was filled with compassion for him; he ran to his son, threw his arms around him and kissed him.

21"The son said to him, 'Father, I have sinned against heaven and against you. I am no longer worthy to be called your son.'

22"But the father said to his servants, 'Quick! Bring the best robe and put it on him. Put a ring on his finger and sandals on his feet. 23Bring the fattened calf and kill it. Let's have a feast and celebrate. 24For this son of mine was dead and is alive again; he was lost and is found.' So they began to celebrate.

25"Meanwhile, the older son was in the field. When he came near the house, he heard music and dancing. 26So he called one of the servants and asked him what was going on. 27'Your brother has come,' he replied, 'and your father has killed the fattened calf because he has him back safe and sound.'

28"The older brother became angry and refused to go in. So his father went out and pleaded with him. 29But he answered his father, 'Look! All these years I've been slaving for you and never disobeyed your orders. Yet you never gave me even a young goat so I could celebrate with my friends. 30But when this son of yours who has squandered your property with prostitutes comes home, you kill the fattened calf for him!'

31"'My son,' the father said, 'you are always with me, and everything I have is yours. 32But we had to celebrate and be glad, because this brother of yours was dead and is alive again; he was lost and is found.'"

Your SOAP—day 15

Scripture: _____

_____

_____

_____

Observation: _____

_____

_____

_____

Application: _____

_____

_____

_____

Prayer: _____

_____

_____

_____

day sixteen

Mark 15

Everything we have learned so far has brought us to this point. We have learned that God sent his son into the world to save it. We learned that we can have a personal relationship with God. We learned that salvation comes through us putting our faith in Christ and following him instead of trying to be "good enough," which we could

www.nextlevelchurch.com/day16

never be. We also learned that God has a plan for each of us and wants to help us in every aspect of our lives.

All of this was made possible because of an event that changed history. This event would make salvation possible. This event is the death and resurrection of Jesus Christ. This is that story.

As you write your SOAP, do your best to understand all that Christ did and experienced for us.

Mark 15 ¹Very early in the morning, the chief priests, with the elders, the teachers of the law and the whole Sanhedrin made their plans. So they bound Jesus, led him away and handed him over to Pilate.

²"Are you the king of the Jews?" asked Pilate.

"You have said so," Jesus replied.

³The chief priests accused him of many things. ⁴So again Pilate asked him, "Aren't you going to answer?

See how many things they are accusing you of."

⁵But Jesus still made no reply, and Pilate was amazed. ⁶Now it was the custom at the festival to release a prisoner whom the people requested. ⁷A man called Barabbas was in prison with the insurrectionists who had committed murder in the uprising. ⁸The crowd came up and asked Pilate to do for them what he usually did.

⁹"Do you want me to release to you the king of the Jews?" asked Pilate, ¹⁰knowing it was out of self-interest that the chief priests had handed Jesus over to him. ¹¹But the chief priests stirred up the crowd to have Pilate release Barabbas instead.

¹²"What shall I do, then, with the one you call the king of the Jews?" Pilate asked them.

¹³"Crucify him!" they shouted.

¹⁴"Why? What crime has he committed?" asked Pilate.

But they shouted all the louder, "Crucify him!"

¹⁵Wanting to satisfy the crowd, Pilate released Barabbas to them. He had Jesus flogged, and handed him over to be crucified.

¹⁶The soldiers led Jesus away into the palace (that is, the Praetorium) and called together the whole company of soldiers. ¹⁷They put a purple robe on him, then twisted together a crown of thorns and set it on him. ¹⁸And they began to call out to him, "Hail, king of the Jews!" ¹⁹Again and again they struck him on the head with a staff and spit on him. Falling on their knees, they paid homage to him. ²⁰And when they had mocked him, they took off the purple robe and put his own clothes on him. Then they led him out to crucify him.

21A certain man from Cyrene, Simon, the father of Alexander and Rufus, was passing by on his way in from the country, and they forced him to carry the cross. 22They brought Jesus to the place called Golgotha (which means "the place of the skull"). 23Then they offered him wine mixed with myrrh, but he did not take it. 24And they crucified him. Dividing up his clothes, they cast lots to see what each would get. 25It was nine in the morning when they crucified him. 26The written notice of the charge against him read: THE KING OF THE JEWS.

27They crucified two rebels with him, one on his right and one on his left. [28][a] 29Those who passed by hurled insults at him, shaking their heads and saying, "So! You who are going to destroy the temple and build it in three days," 30"Come down from the cross and save yourself!"

31In the same way the chief priests and the teachers of the law mocked him among themselves. "He saved others," they said, "but he can't save himself! 32Let this Messiah, this king of Israel, come down now from the cross, that we may see and believe." Those crucified with him also heaped insults on him.

33At noon, darkness came over the whole land until three in the afternoon. 34And at three in the afternoon Jesus cried out in a loud voice, "Eloi, Eloi, lema sabachthani?" (which means, "My God, my God, why have you forsaken me?").

35When some of those standing near heard this, they said, "Listen, he's calling Elijah."

36Someone ran, filled a sponge with wine vinegar, put it on a staff, and offered it to Jesus to drink. "Now leave him alone. Let's see if Elijah comes to take him down," he said.

37With a loud cry, Jesus breathed his last.

38The curtain of the temple was torn in two from top to bottom. 39And when the centurion, who stood there in front of Jesus, saw how he died, he said, "Surely this man was the Son of God!"

40Some women were watching from a distance. Among them were Mary Magdalene, Mary the mother of James the younger and of Joseph, and Salome. 41In Galilee these women had followed him and cared for his needs. Many other women who had come up with him to Jerusalem were also there.

42It was Preparation Day (that is, the day before the Sabbath). So as evening approached, 43Joseph of Arimathea, a prominent member of the Council, who was himself waiting for the kingdom of God, went boldly to Pilate and asked for Jesus' body. 44Pilate was surprised to hear that he was already dead. Summoning the centurion, he asked him if Jesus had already died. 45When he learned from the centurion that it was so, he gave the body to Joseph. 46So Joseph bought some linen cloth, took down the body, wrapped it in the linen, and placed it in a tomb cut out of rock. Then he rolled a stone against the entrance of the tomb. 47Mary Magdalene and Mary the mother of Joseph saw where he was laid.

Your SOAP—day 16

Scripture: _____

_____

_____

_____

Observation: _____

_____

_____

_____

Application: _____

_____

_____

_____

Prayer: _____

_____

_____

_____

_____

The story of the Resurrection of Jesus Christ . . .

Matthew 28 ¹After the Sabbath, at dawn on the first day of the week, Mary Magdalene and the other Mary went to look at the tomb.

²There was a violent earthquake, for an angel of the Lord came down from heaven and, going to the tomb, rolled back the stone and sat on it. ³His appearance was like lightning, and his clothes were white as snow. ⁴The guards were so afraid of him that they shook and became like dead men.

⁵The angel said to the women, "Do not be afraid, for I know that you are looking for Jesus, who was crucified. ⁶He is not here; he has risen, just as he said. Come and see the place where he lay. 7 Then go quickly and tell his disciples: 'He has risen from the dead and is going ahead of you into Galilee. There you will see him.' Now I have told you."

⁸So the women hurried away from the tomb, afraid yet filled with joy, and ran to tell his disciples. ⁹Suddenly Jesus met them. "Greetings," he said. They came to him, clasped his feet and worshiped him. ¹⁰Then Jesus said to them, "Do not be afraid. Go and tell my brothers to go to Galilee; there they will see me."

11While the women were on their way, some of the guards went into the city and reported to the chief priests everything that had happened. 12When the chief priests had met with the elders and devised a plan, they gave the soldiers a large sum of money, 13telling them, "You are to say, 'His disciples came during the night and stole him away while we were asleep.' 14If this report gets to the governor, we will satisfy him and keep you out of trouble." 15So the soldiers took the money and did as they were instructed. And this story has been widely circulated among the Jews to this very day.

16Then the eleven disciples went to Galilee, to the mountain where Jesus had told them to go. 17When they saw him, they worshiped him; but some doubted. 18Then Jesus came to them and said, "All authority in heaven and on earth has been given to me. 19Therefore go and make disciples of all nations, baptizing them in the name of the Father and of the Son and of the Holy Spirit, 20and teaching them to obey everything I have commanded you. And surely I am with you always, to the very end of the age."

Your SOAP—day 17

Scripture: _____

_____

_____

_____

Observation: _____

_____

_____

_____

Application: _____

_____

_____

_____

Prayer: _____

_____

_____

_____

day eighteen
Daniel 3

We are going back in time for this next SOAP as we go to a book in the Old Testament called Daniel. The book of Daniel takes place around the year 600 B.C. At this time in history, Israel (Jewish nation) had been conquered by the Babylonians. This meant that the Jews were either scattered into different surrounding nations,

www.nextlevelchurch.com/day18

or they lost all their rights as they stayed in this now-conquered nation.

The book of Daniel tells the story of a handful of Jewish young men and how God used their faith and their example to impact an entire nation.

Daniel 3 ¹King Nebuchadnezzar made an image of gold, sixty cubits high and six cubits wide, and set it up on the plain of Dura in the province of Babylon. ²He then summoned the satraps, prefects, governors, advisers, treasurers, judges, magistrates and all the other provincial officials to come to the dedication of the image he had set up. ³So the satraps, prefects, governors, advisers, treasurers, judges, magistrates and all the other provincial officials assembled for the dedication of the image that King Nebuchadnezzar had set up, and they stood before it.

⁴Then the herald loudly proclaimed, "Nations and peoples of every language, this is what you are commanded to do: ⁵As soon as you hear the sound of the horn, flute, zither, lyre, harp, pipe and all kinds of music, you must fall down and worship the image of gold that King Nebuchadnezzar has set up. ⁶Whoever does not fall down and worship will immediately be thrown into a blazing furnace."

⁷Therefore, as soon as they heard the sound of the horn, flute, zither, lyre, harp and all kinds of music, all the nations and peoples of every language fell down and worshiped the image of gold that King Nebuchadnezzar had set up.

⁸At this time some astrologers came forward and denounced the Jews. ⁹They said to King Nebuchadnezzar, "May the king live forever! ¹⁰Your Majesty has issued a decree that everyone who hears the sound of the horn, flute, zither, lyre, harp, pipe and all kinds of music must fall down and worship the image of gold, ¹¹and that whoever does not fall down and worship will be thrown into a blazing furnace. ¹²But there are some Jews whom you have set over the affairs of the province of Babylon—Shadrach, Meshach and Abednego—who pay no attention to you, Your Majesty. They neither serve your gods nor worship the image of gold you have set up."

¹³Furious with rage, Nebuchadnezzar summoned Shadrach, Meshach and Abednego. So these men were brought before the king, ¹⁴and Nebuchadnezzar said to them, "Is it true, Shadrach, Meshach and Abednego, that you do not serve my gods or worship the image of gold I have set up?

15Now when you hear the sound of the horn, flute, zither, lyre, harp, pipe and all kinds of music, if you are ready to fall down and worship the image I made, very good. But if you do not worship it, you will be thrown immediately into a blazing furnace. Then what god will be able to rescue you from my hand?" 16Shadrach, Meshach and Abednego replied to him, "King Nebuchadnezzar, we do not need to defend ourselves before you in this matter. 17If we are thrown into the blazing furnace, the God we serve is able to deliver us from it, and he will deliver us from Your Majesty's hand. 18But even if he does not, we want you to know, Your Majesty, that we will not serve your gods or worship the image of gold you have set up."

19Then Nebuchadnezzar was furious with Shadrach, Meshach and Abednego, and his attitude toward them changed. He ordered the furnace heated seven times hotter than usual 20and commanded some of the strongest soldiers in his army to tie up Shadrach, Meshach and Abednego and throw them into the blazing furnace. 21So these men, wearing their robes, trousers, turbans and other clothes, were bound and thrown into the blazing furnace. 22The king's command was so urgent and the furnace so hot that the flames of the fire killed the soldiers who took up Shadrach, Meshach and Abednego, 23and these three men, firmly tied, fell into the blazing furnace.

24Then King Nebuchadnezzar leaped to his feet in amazement and asked his advisers, "Weren't there three men that we tied up and threw into the fire?" They replied, "Certainly, Your Majesty."

25He said, "Look! I see four men walking around in the fire, unbound and unharmed, and the fourth looks like a son of the gods."

26Nebuchadnezzar then approached the opening of the blazing furnace and shouted, "Shadrach, Meshach and Abednego, servants of the Most High God, come out! Come here!"

So Shadrach, Meshach and Abednego came out of the fire, 27and the satraps, prefects, governors and royal advisers crowded around them. They saw that the fire had not harmed their bodies, nor was a hair of their heads singed; their robes were not scorched, and there was no smell of fire on them.

28Then Nebuchadnezzar said, "Praise be to the God of Shadrach, Meshach and Abednego, who has sent his angel and rescued his servants! They trusted in him and defied the king's command and were willing to give up their lives rather than serve or worship any god except their own God. 29Therefore I decree that the people of any nation or language who say anything against the God of Shadrach, Meshach and Abednego be cut into pieces and their houses be turned into piles of rubble, for no other god can save in this way."

30Then the king promoted Shadrach, Meshach and Abednego in the province of Babylon.

Your SOAP—day 18

Scripture: _____

_____

_____

_____

Observation: _____

_____

_____

_____

_____

Application: _____

_____

_____

_____

_____

Prayer: _____

_____

_____

_____

_____

day nineteen
1 Samuel 17

Today we look at another great story in the Old Testament. This time we are in the book of 1 Samuel. Here we find another story of the nation of Israel, but

www.nextlevelchurch.com/day19

this time it is earlier in their history and they are under the leadership of their very first king, King Saul. He was not a good king, but in this story we see a character emerging by the name of David who would become a hero of the nation and eventually become king. This is the story of David fighting the most powerful and notorious warrior in the Philistine army. His name was Goliath.

1 Samuel 17 ¹Now the Philistines gathered their forces for war and assembled at Sokoh in Judah. They pitched camp at Ephes Dammim, between Sokoh and Azekah. ²Saul and the Israelites assembled and camped in the Valley of Elah and drew up their battle line to meet the Philistines. ³The Philistines occupied one hill and the Israelites another, with the valley between them.

⁴A champion named Goliath, who was from Gath, came out of the Philistine camp. His height was six cubits and a span. ⁵He had a bronze helmet on his head and wore a coat of scale armor of bronze

weighing five thousand shekels; 6On his legs he wore bronze greaves, and a bronze javelin was slung on his back. 7His spear shaft was like a weaver's rod, and its iron point weighed six hundred shekels. His shield bearer went ahead of him.

8Goliath stood and shouted to the ranks of Israel, "Why do you come out and line up for battle? Am I not a Philistine, and are you not the servants of Saul? Choose a man and have him come down to me. 9 If he is able to fight and kill me, we will become your subjects; but if I overcome him and kill him, you will become our subjects and serve us." 10Then the Philistine said, "This day I defy the armies of Israel! Give me a man and let us fight each other." 11On hearing the Philistine's words, Saul and all the Israelites were dismayed and terrified.

12Now David was the son of an Ephrathite named Jesse, who was from Bethlehem in Judah. Jesse had eight sons, and in Saul's time he was very old. 13Jesse's three oldest sons had followed Saul to the war: The firstborn was Eliab; the second, Abinadab; and the third, Shammah. 14David was the youngest. The three oldest followed Saul, 15but David went back and forth from Saul to tend his father's sheep at Bethlehem.

16For forty days the Philistine came forward every morning and evening and took his stand.

17Now Jesse said to his son David, "Take this ephah of roasted grain and these ten loaves of bread for your brothers and hurry to their camp. 18Take along these ten cheeses to the commander of their unit. See how your brothers are and bring back some assurance from them. 19They are with Saul and all the men of

Israel in the Valley of Elah, fighting against the Philistines."

20Early in the morning David left the flock in the care of a shepherd, loaded up and set out, as Jesse had directed. He reached the camp as the army was going out to its battle positions, shouting the war cry. 21Israel and the Philistines were drawing up their lines facing each other. 22David left his things with the keeper of supplies, ran to the battle lines and asked his brothers how they were. 23As he was talking with them, Goliath, the Philistine champion from Gath, stepped out from his lines and shouted his usual defiance, and David heard it. 24Whenever the Israelites saw the man, they all fled from him in great fear.

25Now the Israelites had been saying, "Do you see how this man keeps coming out? He comes out to defy Israel. The king will give great wealth to the man who kills him. He will also give him his daughter in marriage and will exempt his family from taxes in Israel."

26David asked the men standing near him, "What will be done for the man who kills this Philistine and removes this disgrace from Israel? Who is this uncircumcised Philistine that he should defy the armies of the living God?"

27They repeated to him what they had been saying and told him, "This is what will be done for the man who kills him."

28When Eliab, David's oldest brother, heard him speaking with the men, he burned with anger at him and asked, "Why have you come down here? And with whom did you leave those few sheep in the wilderness? I know how conceited you are and how wicked your heart is; you came down only to watch the battle."

29"Now what have I done?" said David. "Can't I even speak?" 30He then turned away to someone else and brought up the same matter, and the men answered him as before. 31What David said was overheard and reported to Saul, and Saul sent for him.

32David said to Saul, "Let no one lose heart on account of this Philistine; your servant will go and fight him."

33Saul replied, "You are not able to go out against this Philistine and fight him; you are only a young man, and he has been a warrior from his youth."

34But David said to Saul, "Your servant has been keeping his father's sheep. When a lion or a bear came and carried off a sheep from the flock, 35I went after it, struck it and rescued the sheep from its mouth. When it turned on me, I seized it by its hair, struck it and killed it. 36Your servant has killed both the lion and the bear; this uncircumcised Philistine will be like one of them, because he has defied the armies of the living God. 37The LORD who rescued me from the paw of the lion and the paw of the bear will rescue me from the hand of this Philistine."

Saul said to David, "Go, and the LORD be with you." 38Then Saul dressed David in his own tunic. He put a coat of armor on him and a bronze helmet on his head. 39David fastened on his sword over the tunic and tried walking around, because he was not used to them.

"I cannot go in these," he said to Saul, "because I am not used to them." So he took them off. 40Then he took his staff in his hand, chose five smooth stones from the stream, put them in the pouch of his shepherd's bag and, with his sling in his hand, approached the Philistine.

41Meanwhile, the Philistine, with his shield bearer in front of him, kept coming closer to David. 42He looked David over and saw that he was little more than a boy, glowing with health and handsome, and he despised him. 43He said to David, "Am I a dog, that you come at me with sticks?" And the Philistine cursed David by his gods. 44"Come here," he said, "and I'll give your flesh to the birds and the wild animals!"

45David said to the Philistine, "You come against me with sword and spear and javelin, but I come against you in the name of the LORD Almighty, the God of the armies of Israel, whom you have defied. 46This day the LORD will deliver you into my hands, and I'll strike you down and cut off your head. This very day I will give the carcasses of the Philistine army to the birds and the wild animals, and the whole world will know that there is a God in Israel. 47All those gathered here will know that it is not by sword or spear that the LORD saves; for the battle is the LORD's, and he will give all of you into our hands."

48As the Philistine moved closer to attack him, David ran quickly toward the battle line to meet him. 49Reaching into his bag and taking out a stone, he slung it and struck the Philistine on the forehead. The stone sank into his forehead, and he fell facedown on the ground.

50So David triumphed over the Philistine with a sling and a stone; without a sword in his hand he struck down the Philistine and killed him.

51David ran and stood over him. He took hold of the Philistine's sword and drew it from the sheath. After he killed him, he cut off his head with the sword.

When the Philistines saw that their hero was dead, they turned and ran. 52Then the men of Israel and Judah surged forward with a shout and pursued the Philistines to the entrance of Gath and to the gates of Ekron. Their dead were strewn along the Shaaraim road to Gath and Ekron. 53When the Israelites returned from chasing the Philistines, they plundered their camp.

54David took the Philistine's head and brought it to Jerusalem; he put the Philistine's weapons in his own tent.

55As Saul watched David going out to meet the Philistine, he said to Abner, commander of the army, "Abner, whose son is that young man?"

Abner replied, "As surely as you live, Your Majesty, I don't know."

56The king said, "Find out whose son this young man is."

57As soon as David returned from killing the Philistine, Abner took him and brought him before Saul, with David still holding the Philistine's head.

58"Whose son are you, young man?" Saul asked him. David said, "I am the son of your servant Jesse of Bethlehem."

Your SOAP—day 19

Scripture: _____

_____

_____

_____

Observation: _____

_____

_____

_____

_____

Application: _____

_____

_____

_____

_____

Prayer: _____

_____

_____

_____

_____

I n this soap, we are going to look at the book of Psalms. This book is in the Old Testament and is written differ-ently than some of the historical or instructional books we have been in thus far. This book is actually a collec-tion of songs and poetry. This may at first seem a little different, but music and song have always played an important

www.nextlevelchurch.com/day20

role in the church and our worship of God.

As a book of poetry and songs, Psalms is full of metaphors and analogies that are not necessarily meant to be taken at face value. Make sure you look at the heart of the message being conveyed through these songs.

Just so you know. The Psalm we are going to SOAP about was actually written by David, the warrior king introduced in our last SOAP.

Psalm 23 1The LORD is my shepherd, I lack nothing. 2He makes me lie down in green pastures, he leads me beside quiet waters, 3He refreshes my soul. He guides me along the right paths for his name's sake. 4Even though I walk through the darkest valley, I will fear no evil, for you are with me; your rod and your staff, they comfort me.

⁵You prepare a table before me in the presence of my enemies. You anoint my head with oil; my cup overflows. ⁶Surely your goodness and love will follow me all the days of my life, and I will dwell in the house of the LORD forever.

Your SOAP—day 20

Scripture: _____

_____

_____

_____

Observation: _____

_____

_____

_____

_____

Application: _____

_____

_____

_____

_____

Prayer: _____

_____

_____

_____

_____

Psalm 91 ¹Whoever dwells in the shelter of the Most High will rest in the shadow of the Almighty.

²I will say of the LORD, "He is my refuge and my fortress, my God, in whom I trust."

³Surely he will save you from the fowler's snare and from the deadly pestilence. ⁴He will cover you with his feathers, and under his wings you will find refuge; his faithfulness will be your shield and rampart. ⁵You will not fear the terror of night, nor the arrow that flies by day, ⁶Nor the pestilence that stalks in the darkness, nor the plague that destroys at midday. ⁷A thousand may fall at your side, ten thousand at your right hand, but it will not come near you. ⁸You will only observe with your eyes and see the punishment of the wicked. ⁹If you say, "The LORD is my refuge," and you make the Most High your dwelling, ¹⁰No harm will overtake you, no disaster will come near your tent. ¹¹For he will command his angels concerning you to guard you in all your ways; ¹²They will lift you up in their hands, so that you will not strike your foot against a stone. ¹³You will tread on the lion and the cobra; you will trample the great lion and the serpent.

¹⁴"Because he loves me," says the LORD, "I will rescue him; I will protect him, for he acknowledges my name. ¹⁵He will call on me, and I will answer

him; I will be with him in trouble, I will deliver him and honor him. [16]With long life I will satisfy him and show him my salvation."

Your SOAP—day 21

Scripture: _____

_____

_____

Observation: _____

_____

_____

_____

Application: _____

_____

_____

_____

Prayer: _____

_____

_____

_____

Now that you have completed our introduction to SOAP, we encourage you to get one of our SOAP Reading Guides and start to follow the passages listed.

www.nextlevelchurch.com/
nextsteps

We hope this book has helped you gain an understanding and confidence in reading the greatest book in history—the wonderful Word of God—the Bible. Our prayer is that this is just the beginning of your interactions with the God of the universe who desires to meet with *you*!